Step-by-Step
Tasty Curries

igloobooks

Published in 2013
by Igloo Books Ltd
Cottage Farm
Sywell
Northants
NN6 0BJ
www.igloobooks.com

Food photography and recipe development: PhotoCuisine UK
Front and back cover images © PhotoCuisine UK

OCE001 0813
4 6 8 10 9 7 5 3
ISBN: 978-0-85780-689-5

Printed and manufactured in China

Step-by-Step
Tasty Curries

Contents

Thai Green Curry

Ingredients

For the spice paste:
1 tsp coriander seeds
½ tsp cumin seeds
4 cardamom pods
100 g / 3 ½ oz coriander stalks
1 small onion, peeled and chopped
2 green chillies
5 cloves of garlic, peeled
2.5 cm / 1" fresh root ginger
pinch ground cloves
½ tsp ground cinnamon

To finish:
2 tbsp vegetable oil
1 onion, peeled and chopped
4 chicken thighs, skinned
250 ml / 9 fl. oz / 1 cup water
125 g / 4 ½ oz / ½ cup baby corn
juice of ½ lemon

SERVES 4 | PREP TIME 5 minutes | COOKING TIME 50 minutes

Grind the whole spices in a pestle and mortar.
Blend the ingredients for the spice paste in a food processor
until smooth, adding a little water if necessary.

Heat the oil in a pan and fry the onion until golden.

Add the paste and cook for about 10 minutes, stirring and adding a little water to stop it burning if necessary.

Add the chicken thighs and the water and cook over a low heat until the chicken is cooked – about 30 minutes.

Add the baby corn and cook gently for a few minutes, ensuring they are coated with the sauce.

Reduce the sauce if necessary, then adjust the seasoning and add the lemon juice. Serve with basmati rice .

Mango Lassi

Ingredients

500 ml / 1 pint / 2 cups plain yoghurt

2-3 mangoes, peeled and stoned

400 ml / 13 fl. oz / 1 ½ cups water

2-3 tbsp sugar

juice of ½ lime

1 lime quartered for garnish

salt

ice cubes

SERVES 4 | PREP TIME 10 minutes

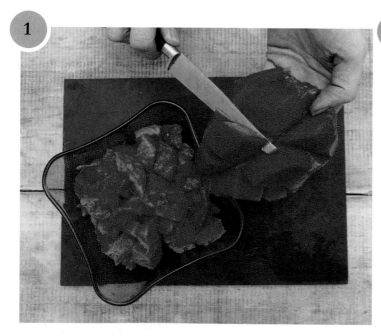

Peel, stone and dice the mangoes into chunks.

Add the yoghurt, water, sugar and lime juice to a blender and blend.

Add the mangoes to the blender and blend. Transfer the mixture back to the jug.

Add a little more sugar and lime juice to taste.

Add a pinch of salt and mix well.

Serve immediately in small bowls or glasses, over ice.

Pork Biryani

Ingredients

4 tbsp groundnut oil

450 g / 1 lb / 2 cups pork shoulder, diced

2 onions, peeled and finely chopped

2 cloves of garlic, chopped

4 cardamom pods

4 cloves

1 cinnamon stick

1 tsp garam masala

½ tsp turmeric

pinch of saffron

250 ml 9 fl. oz / 1 cup water

75 g / 2 ½ oz / ⅓ cup cooked peas

500 g / 1 lb / 2 cups basmati rice

fresh coriander

SERVES 6 | **PREP TIME** 15 minutes | **COOKING TIME** 60-70 minutes

Heat the oil in a pan, add the pork and cook until golden brown.

Add the onions and cardamom and cook until golden.

3

Mix in the rest of the spices and coat the chicken.

4

Add the water and leave to cook gently for about 20 minutes.

5

Then add the peas and stir well. Meanwhile, cook the rice according to packet instructions.

6

Drain and add the rice to the pan, stir well and leave to cook gently for 15 minutes. Adjust the seasoning and serve warm, sprinkled with chopped coriander.

Curried Rice Salad

Ingredients

2 tbsp vegetable oil

1 tsp mustard seeds

¼ tsp fenugreek seeds

1 red chilli, finely chopped

1 tsp fresh root ginger, grated

300 g / 10 oz / 1 ¼ cups basmati
rice, cooked

juice of ½ lemon

salt

2 tomatoes

200 g / 7oz white crab meat

½ cucumber, finely chopped

SERVES 6 | PREP TIME 15 minutes | COOKING TIME 60-70 minutes

Heat the oil in a pan and add the spices and stir-fry briefly.

Add the ginger and cook for another 30 seconds.

Add the rice and lemon juice and cook through. Season and set aside.

Plunge the tomatoes into boiling water for 20 seconds, remove and then peel. Cut them in half, scoop out and discard the seeds, then dice the flesh.

Mix the crab, tomato concasse and cucumber into the pilaff and adjust the seasoning.

Serve with an extra squeeze of lemon juice.

Vegetable Curry

Ingredients

50 ml / 3 ½ fl. oz / ½ cup water

2 tbsp desiccated coconut, soaked in water

2 tbsp vegetable oil

1 tsp cumin seeds

1 onion, peeled and sliced

2 green chillies, halved

½ tsp turmeric

1 aubergine, diced

3 shallots

2 red peppers, deseeded and chopped

1 large courgette, diced

1 head of broccoli, cut into florets

150 g / 5 oz / 1 cup button mushrooms, thickly sliced

1 tbsp fresh ginger, grated

10 curry leaves

6 tbsp plain yoghurt

salt

SERVES 4 | PREP TIME 20 minutes | COOKING TIME 30 minutes

1

Heat the oil in a wok and add the cumin, onion and chillies and cook until the onions are lightly gold.

2

Add the turmeric and the vegetables one at a time, in the order listed, cooking each one for a few minutes before adding the next, allowing them to colour and soften.

Add the water and cook until the vegetables are nearly tender.

Meanwhile blend the ginger with the soaked coconut and shallots to make a paste, using the soaking water to slacken it.

Stir into the curry and cook for a few minutes, then add the curry leaves.

Stir in the yoghurt and heat without boiling. Season and serve warm.

Prawn Curry

Ingredients

For the spice taste:

1-2 red chillies

1 tbsp fresh ginger, grated

4 cloves of garlic, peeled

2 shallots, peeled

1 tsp fennel seeds

1 tsp mustard seeds

juice of ½ lemon

To finish:

500 g / 18 oz / 2 cups raw prawns, with shells

1 head of broccoli, cut into florets

2 tbsp vegetable oil

2 green or red peppers, deseeded and sliced into strips

salt and pepper

juice of 1 lemon

SERVES 4 | PREP TIME 35 minutes | COOKING TIME 10 minutes

Make the spice paste by whizzing all the ingredients in a blender. Add a little salt.

Toss the prawns in the paste and leave to marinate in the refrigerator for 30 minutes.

Lightly cook the broccoli in boiling water until just tender but still slightly crunchy.

Heat the oil in a pan until nearly smoking then add the prawns with their marinade and the peppers and stir-fry briskly for 2 minutes.

Add the broccoli and stir-fry on a medium heat, until the prawns turn pink all over.

Turn onto a serving platter, squeeze over more lemon juice and season. Serve sizzling with finger bowls.

Coconut Shrimp Curry

Ingredients

2 red chillies, deseeded if preferred

1 red onion, peeled and chopped

2 cloves of garlic

1 tbsp vegetable oil

1 tbsp fresh ginger, grated

1 tsp fennel seeds

½ tsp fenugreek seeds

10 curry leaves

3 kaffir lime leaves

1 tsp turmeric

300 ml / 10 fl. oz / 1 ½ cups coconut milk

100 ml / 3 ½ fl. oz / 1 cup fish stock

1 tbsp tamarind paste

250 g / 10 oz / 1 cup raw prawns, shelled

salt

SERVES 2 | PREP TIME 5-10 minutes | COOKING TIME 15 minutes

Whiz the chillies, onion and garlic in a food processor with a tbsp of water to make a paste.

Heat the oil in a wok and fry off the paste for 2 minutes.

Add the ginger and whole spices and cook until the fragrance fills the kitchen. Stir in the turmeric.

Pour in the coconut milk, fish stock and tamarind paste and stir well. Leave to simmer for 5 minutes.

Add the prawns and cook on a medium heat for 5 minutes until they turn pink.

Adjust the seasoning and serve into bowls or coconut shells.

Chicken Biryani

Ingredients

4 tbsp groundnut oil

4 chicken legs, with skin

2 onions, peeled and finely chopped

4 cardamom pods

2 cloves of garlic, chopped

½ tsp ground ginger

1 tsp garam masala

½ tsp turmeric

pinch of saffron

250 ml / 9 fl. oz / 1 cup water

500 g / 1 lb / 2 cups basmati rice

fresh coriander

SERVES 4 | PREP TIME 10 minutes | COOKING TIME 1 hour

Heat the oil in a pan and add the chicken, skin side down and cook until golden brown.

Add the onions and cardamom pods and cook until golden.

Mix in the rest of the spices and coat the chicken.

Add the water and leave to simmer gently for 40 minutes.

Meanwhile, cook the rice according to packet instructions. Drain and add to the pan, stir well and leave to cook gently for another 10-15 minutes.

Adjust the seasoning, add some fresh coriander and serve onto individual plates.

Lamb Curry

Ingredients

1 tbsp fresh ginger, very finely chopped

8-10 cloves of garlic, peeled and finely chopped

2 tbsp vegetable oil

4 cardamom pods

2 bay leaves

1 onion, peeled and finely chopped

2 red peppers, deseeded and cut into strips

800 g / 1 ¾ lbs / 3 ⅓ cups lamb, cubed

1 red chilli, whole

½ tsp turmeric

1 tsp ground cumin

1 tsp garam masala

½ tsp ground cinnamon

6 tomatoes, finely diced

500 ml / 18 fl. oz / 2 cups water

salt

SERVES 6 | PREP TIME 15 minutes | COOKING TIME 1 hour

Blend the garlic and ginger together with a little water or oil in a pestle and mortar to make a paste.

Heat the oil in a large pan and fry the cardamom pods and bay leaves for a few seconds. Add the onion and peppers. Fry until softened and lightly golden.

Add the lamb and red chilli and stir well.

Next add the ginger paste, spices and a little salt and cook for a few minutes until the lamb is lightly browned.

Add the tomatoes and water and simmer for 45 minutes, until the lamb is completely tender. You may need to top up with water occasionally.

Garnish with coriander and serve hot with basmati rice.

Spiced Rice Purses

Ingredients

2 tbsp vegetable oil

2 bay leaves

3 cardamom pods

8 black peppercorns

1 tsp cumin seeds

2 red chillies

1 onion, peeled and chopped

300 g / 10 oz / 1 ¼ cups cooked basmati rice

8 ripe tomatoes, finely chopped

salt

5 large filo sheets

2 tbsp butter, melted

chive stems

SERVES 4-5 | PREP TIME 30-40 minutes | COOKING TIME 15-20 minutes

Heat the oil in a large pan and add the whole spices and chilli and cook for 30 seconds.

Add the onion and cook until translucent.

3

Stir in the rice and tomatoes, season and stir to heat through. Leave to cool for a few minutes.

4

Preheat the oven to 200°C (180° fan) / 400F / gas 7.

5

Brush the filo pastry sheets with the melted butter and lay out flat.

6

7

Spoon some of the tomato pilaff into the centre of each one, then gather the filo pastry up around to make a parcel.

Use the chive stems to secure the parcel. You could also use cook's string, which should be removed after cooking.

8

Place on a greased baking sheet and bake in the oven for 15-20 minutes or until the pastry is crisp and golden. Tie some fresh chives around each parcel and serve.

Mutton Curry

Ingredients

For the marinade:

150 ml / 5 fl. oz / ⅔ cup plain yoghurt

2 cloves of garlic, crushed

2 tsp fresh ginger, grated

1-2 tsp chilli powder

½ tsp turmeric

For the curry:

800 g / 1 ¾ lb / 3 ⅓ cups mutton, cubed

3 tbsp vegetable oil

1 onion, peeled and sliced

6 cardamom pods

4 cloves

4 tomatoes, finely chopped

½ tsp caraway seeds

½ tsp ground cinnamon

700 ml / 25 fl. oz / 3 cups water

2 potatoes, peeled and diced

salt

SERVES 4 | PREP TIME 5 minutes | COOKING TIME 2 hours

Whisk all of the ingredients for the marinade together.

Coat the meat in the marinade thoroughly. Chill in the refrigerator for at least 2 hours.

3

Heat the oil in a pan and fry the onions until deep gold, for about 10 minutes, careful not to burn them.

4

Add the whole spices and cook for 1 minute, stirring continuously.

5

Add the meat and reduce the heat and cook for 10 minutes, until the marinade is absorbed.

Cook briskly for 5 minutes, then add the tomatoes and mix well, stirring continuously.

Add the caraway and cinnamon and mix.

Next add water and leave to cook for at least 1 ½ hours or until the meat is tender.

Twenty minutes before the end of cooking time add the potatoes and stir well. You may need to add more water. Season and serve.

Spiced Crab

Ingredients

2 tbsp vegetable oil

1 tsp mustard seeds

1 tsp fennel seeds

½ tsp turmeric

1 tsp cumin seeds

1-2 red chillies, deseeded if preferred

1 tsp fresh ginger, finely chopped

2 celery stalks, peeled and finely chopped

1 fennel bulb, trimmed and finely chopped

500 g / 18 oz / 1 cup white crab meat

salt

50 ml / 2 fl. oz / ¼ cup water

juice of 1 lime or lemon

SERVES 4 | PREP TIME 10 minutes | COOKING TIME 10-15 minutes

Heat the oil in a pan and add the spices. Cook until the seeds start to pop and the aroma fills the kitchen.

Add the chillies and ginger and cook for a further 2 minutes.

Add the celery and fennel and sauté briskly until just tender.

Stir in the crab meat, season with salt and stir to mix the ingredients well.

Add water and allow it to reduce to a coating consistency.

Just before serving, squeeze in the lime juice and adjust the seasoning if necessary.

Tofu Curry

Ingredients

400 g / 13 oz / 1 ½ cups extra firm tofu, cubed

2 tbsp garam masala or curry paste

1 red or green chilli, seeded if desired and finely chopped

3 tbsp groundnut oil

1 onion, peeled and finely chopped

250 g / 9 oz / 1 cup button mushrooms

200 ml / 6 ½ fl. oz / ¾ cup coconut milk

1 tbsp fish sauce

juice of 1 lime

salt and pepper

SERVES 4 | PREP TIME 20 minutes | COOKING TIME 15 minutes

Prepare and measure all of the ingredients. Slice the onions and mushrooms in half and dice the tofu.

Toss the tofu with the garam masala or curry paste and chilli and leave for 15 minutes. Heat the oil in a pan and add the onion and tofu and cook over a high heat.

Cook for a few minutes until the onion is translucent and the tofu is crisping on all sides. Don't over-stir the tofu, as it will break up. Make sure the tofu is crisp before proceeding to the next step.

Add the mushrooms and cook on a high heat until golden on all sides. Season generously and cook for a further minute.

Add the coconut milk and mix well to coat the ingredients.

Mix in the fish sauce and leave to simmer for 5 minutes. Squeeze in the lime juice and season before serving.

Turnip and Shrimp Curry

Ingredients

2 tbsp butter

1 onion, peeled and chopped

1 clove of garlic, chopped

1 tsp garam masala

3 curry leaves

2 turnips, peeled and finely chopped

4 celery stalks, peeled and finely chopped

400 g / 14 oz / 2 cups chopped tomatoes

300 ml / 10 fl. oz / 1 ¼ cups vegetable stock

1 tsp paprika (sweet or hot)

250 g / 9 oz / ¾ cup prawns, shelled and cooked

300 g / 10 oz / 1 ¼ cups spinach leaves, washed

salt and pepper

SERVES 4 | PREP TIME 20 minutes | COOKING TIME 35 minutes

Heat the butter in a large pan and fry the onion and garlic until golden.

Add the garam masala and curry leaves and cook for 1 minute. Stir in the turnips and celery and coat in the spices.

Pour in the tomatoes, blending them with a wooden spoon.

Pour in the stock and stir well. Sprinkle with paprika and leave to simmer for 25 minutes or until the turnips are tender.

Stir in the prawns and warm through for a few minutes.

Stir in the spinach leaves. Season well and serve hot.

Meatball Curry

Ingredients

For the paste:

1 tbsp coriander seeds

1 tbsp cumin seeds

½ tbsp black peppercorns

2-4 green chillies

8 cloves of garlic, peeled

2 stalks lemongrass

1 bunch of coriander roots

2 tbsp fresh galangal or ginger

3 kaffir lime leaves

6 shallots, peeled

1 tbsp dried shrimp paste

For the meatballs:

500 g / 1 lb / 2 cups mixed minced beef

1 onion, peeled and finely chopped

2 cloves of garlic, crushed

1 tsp ground coriander

For the sauce:

400 ml / 13 ½ fl. oz / 1 ½ cups coconut milk

200 ml / 7 fl. oz / ¾ cup chicken stock

4 green tomatoes, halved

1 tbsp tamarind paste

1-2 tbsp fish sauce

1-2 tbsp caster (superfine) sugar

juice of 1-2 limes, Thai basil

SERVES 4 | PREP TIME 30 minutes | COOKING TIME 35 minutes

To make the curry paste, pound the seeds in a pestle and mortar until finely ground.

Tip into a food processor and whiz with the rest of the ingredients until smooth. You will only need 4-5 tbsp for this recipe, so keep the rest in a sealed jar in the fridge.

3

Make the meatballs by thoroughly combining all the ingredients, then roll them into small walnut-size balls. Refrigerate for 30 minutes to firm up.

4

Brown the meatballs in an oiled pan; this will help them hold together when poaching.

5

Heat the spice paste in a wok with 2 tbsp of the cream from the top of the coconut milk, until sizzling.

6

Pour in the coconut milk, chicken stock and stir in the tamarind paste, fish sauce and sugar.

Arrange on a greased baking sheet and warm for 5 minutes in the oven, then leave to drain upside down again while you prepare the stuffing.

Heat the oil in a large pan and fry the onion until softened.

Then add the garlic and rice and stir well.

Add the spices and stir to coat the rice.

Stir over a medium heat for 2 minutes or until fragrant.

Season and then pour over the stock. Cover with a lid and cook gently for about 15 minutes or until the rice has absorbed all the liquid and is tender. Run a fork through the rice to loosen.

Using a spoon, stuff the tomatoes with the rice mixture, heaping it up to form a dome shape. Replace the tomato tops.

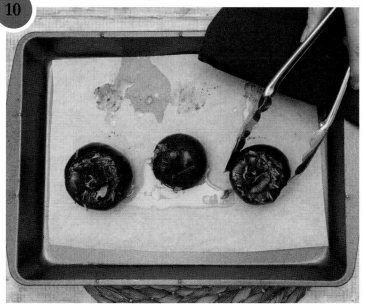

Place in a roasting tin, drizzle over a little oil and bake in the oven for about 30 minutes. Serve warm or cold.

Courgette Cappuccino

Ingredients

1 tbsp butter

1 onion, peeled and sliced

2 cloves of garlic, chopped

1 tsp mustard seeds

1 tsp ground coriander

1 kg / 2 ¼ lbs / 4 ¼ cups courgettes (courgette), sliced

2 floury potatoes, peeled and chopped

1 bunch parsley, chopped

1 bunch coriander, chopped

800 ml / 1 ¾ pints / 3 ⅓ cups vegetable stock

salt and pepper

200 ml / 7 fl. oz / ¾ cup double cream

2 tomatoes

1 tsp smoked paprika

SERVES 4 | PREP TIME 30 minutes | COOKING TIME 30 minutes

Heat the butter in a large pan and fry the onion and garlic gently until golden.

Add the spices and cook until the mustard seeds pop. Add the courgettes, potatoes and herbs and then season.

Pour in the stock. Simmer until the potatoes are tender, and then leave to cool for 10 minutes.

Liquidise in a blender until smooth, then return to the pan and reheat when required. Adjust the seasoning if necessary. For the cappuccino cream, whisk the cream to soft peaks.

Plunge the tomatoes into boiling water for 20 seconds, then remove them and peel. Cut in half and scoop out and discard the seeds, then cut the flesh into diced pieces.

Ladle the soup into small bowls or even coffee cups and spoon over the whipped cream. Sprinkle with the tomato concasse and a little smoked paprika.

Indian Soup

Ingredients

2 tbsp butter

1 onion, peeled and finely chopped

3 cloves of garlic, chopped

2 red chillies, deseeded if preferred, chopped

1 tsp cumin seeds

1 tsp turmeric

1 tsp fennel seeds

1 tsp mustard seeds

1 tbsp tomato puree

6 curry leaves

1.5 l / 2 ½ pints / 5 cups fish stock

2 potatoes, peeled and diced

200 g / 7 oz mussels, cleaned

200 g / 7 oz raw prawns, shelled

150 g / 5 oz firm white fish, cut into chunks

100 g / 3 ½ oz / ½ cup creamed coconut block

juice of 1 lime

SERVES 4 | PREP TIME 30 minutes | COOKING TIME 30 minutes

Heat the butter in a pan and add the onion, garlic and chillies and cook until softened. Add the spices and fry until the mustard seeds pop and the fragrance fills the kitchen.

Stir in the tomato puree and cook for 2 minutes, stirring well. Add the curry leaves and fish stock and simmer for 5 minutes.

Add the potatoes and cook for another 5 minutes.

Add the shellfish and fish, keeping the mussels at the top of the pan, and simmer until the mussels have opened and the prawns have turned pink.

Remove the meat from the mussel shells and return to the pan. Discard any mussels that remain closed.

Grate in the creamed coconut and stir well. Squeeze in the lime juice just before serving. Serve in deep bowls with naan.

Beef Curry

Ingredients

200 ml / 6 ½ fl. oz / ¾ cup basmati rice, rinsed in cold water, then drained

400 ml / 13 ½ fl. oz / 1 ½ cups boiling water

50 ml / 1 ½ fl. oz sunflower oil

400 g / 13 ½ oz / 1 ½ cups beef rump, sliced

1 tbsp fresh ginger, minced

2 cloves garlic, minced

a few slices of fresh ginger

1 tsp ground cumin

1 tsp ground coriander

1 tsp turmeric

1 tsp ground black pepper

½ tsp chilli powder

½ tsp ground ginger

100 g / 3 ½ oz / ½ cup frozen peas

100 ml / 3 ½ fl. oz / ½ cup water

sprigs of coriander, to garnish

salt

SERVES 4 | PREP TIME 25 minutes | COOKING TIME 30 minutes

Add the rice and a little salt to the boiling water in a large saucepan. Bring back to the boil, cover, and simmer for 10-12 minutes. Remove from the heat, keeping the lid on, and set to one side.

Heat the sunflower oil in a large pan over a moderate heat. Quickly sear the beef all over.

Add the minced garlic and ginger as well as the slices of ginger to the dish and sauté for a few minutes, stirring occasionally.

Add the spices to the pan and stir well to combine. Pour in the water and bring the curry to a simmer. Simmer gently for 10 minutes.

Stir in the peas, remove from the heat, and allow the residual heat to cook them. Adjust the seasoning to taste.

Re-heat the rice if necessary and spoon into serving bowls. Spoon the curry on top and garnish with coriander before serving.

Chicken and Squash Curry

Ingredients

3 tbsp vegetable oil

1 onion, peeled and finely sliced

2 cloves of garlic, chopped

1 tsp fresh ginger, grated

1 tsp ground coriander

pinch of turmeric

½ tsp ground cumin

½ tsp garam masala

1 tsp paprika

1 tsp mustard seeds

1 butternut squash, seeded, peeled and chopped

450 g / 1 lb / 2 cups chicken thigh meat, skinned and diced

100 g / 3 ½ oz / ½ cup plain yoghurt

salt

coriander leaves, to garnish

SERVES 4 | **PREP TIME** 15 minutes | **COOKING TIME** 50 minutes

Heat the oil in a pan and sauté the onion for about 10 minutes or until golden-brown.

Add the garlic and ginger and fry for another minute.

Add the spices and stir well.

Add 200 ml of water and cook gently for 10 minutes.

Add the squash and stir well to coat in the spices.

6

7

Add the chicken to the saucepan and top up with 300 ml of water. Cook at a simmer for around 20 minutes until the chicken and squash are tender.

Stir in the yoghurt and heat through, without boiling.

8

Season and sprinkle with coriander leaves before serving.

Monkfish and Pineapple Curry

Ingredients

1 tbsp coriander seeds, crushed

1 tbsp garam masala

1 tbsp ground cumin

2 cloves

3 tbsp groundnut oil

½ pineapple, peeled and diced

1 orange pepper, cut into strips

100 ml / 3 ½ fl. oz / ½ cup coconut milk

200 ml / 6 ½ fl. oz / ¾ cup vegetable stock

1.2 kg / 2 ½ lbs / 5 cups monkfish tail, peeled and cubed

salt

SERVES 6 | PREP TIME 20 minutes | COOKING TIME 30 minutes

Crush the coriander seeds with a pestle and mortar, and then add to the other spices.

Skin the pineapple; remove the core and then slice into chunks.

51

Heat the oil in a pan, then add the spices and cook for a few seconds until the aroma fills the kitchen.

Add the pepper and cook for a few minutes until softened.

Add the pineapple and mix well, blending all of the ingredients.

Simmer gently for a few minutes, ensuring the pineapple is coated well.

Add the stock, season and reduce the heat. Cook for 10 minutes, stirring occasionally.

Add the coconut milk and mix well.

Add the monkfish and cook for 5 minutes, stirring regularly.

When the monkfish is cooked and tender, serve the curry alongside some white basmati rice.

Mozzarella Lollipops

Ingredients

250 g / 9 oz / 1 cup ciliegine mozzarella
pearls, drained
20 lollipop sticks

8 cardamom pods
1 tsp turmeric
2 tsp ground coriander
2 tsp ground cumin
1 tsp ground ginger
2 tbsp sea salt

SERVES 16-20 | PREP TIME 15 minutes

1

Measure and prepare all of the ingredients. Drain the mozzarella pearls and place in a bowl.

2

To make the spice salt, pound the cardamom pods in a pestle and mortar, removing the husks and grinding the seeds to a fine powder.

Mix with the ground coriander, cumin and ginger.

Mix in the turmeric and grind to ensure all of the spices blend well.

Brush the mozzarella pearls with the spice salt just before serving, otherwise the salt will dissolve on the cheese.

Push onto the lollipop sticks and serve.

Hot Chicken Curry

Ingredients

1 tsp mustard seeds

1 tsp fenugreek seeds

1 tsp cumin seeds

50 ml / 1 ½ fl. oz sunflower oil

1 onion, finely chopped

2 cloves garlic, finely chopped

1 red chilli, de-seeded and sliced

2 tsp coriander seeds

1 tsp chilli powder

1 tsp garam masala

1 tsp caster sugar

400 ml / 13 ½ fl. oz / 1 ½ cups coconut milk

4 skinless chicken breasts, diced

salt and pepper

toasted naan bread, to garnish

juice of ½ lemon, to taste

coriander leaves, to garnish

SERVES 4 | PREP TIME 25 minutes | COOKING TIME 40 minutes

Heat a large frying pan over a moderate heat until hot, then add the cumin, coriander, fenugreek and mustard seeds and toast for one minute.

Remove from the heat and grind into a powder using a pestle and mortar.

Heat the olive oil in a casserole dish over a moderate heat and sweat the onion for 4-5 minutes until soft. Add the garlic and continue to cook, stirring occasionally for 3-4 minutes.

Add the ground spices, the chilli powder, garam masala, sugar and 1 tsp of salt, stir well, and cook for 1-2 minutes.

Add the chopped chilli and stir well to combine all of the spices.

Add the coconut milk and 100 ml of water to the dish and bring to a simmer.

Add the chicken and simmer for 12-15 minutes until it is cooked. Adjust the seasoning using salt, pepper and lemon juice.

Heat the oven to 180°C (160° fan) 375F, gas 5. Place the naan bread on a baking tray heat in the oven for 5 minutes.

Spoon the curry into bowls and garnish with coriander leaves and slices of naan bread. Serve alongside basmati rice.

Potato Curry

Ingredients

50 ml / 1 ½ fl. oz / ¼ cup sunflower oil

2 large aubergines, diced

1 tsp black poppy seeds

1 large red chilli, cut in half

1 onion, finely chopped

2 cloves garlic, minced

1 tsp ground cumin, 1 tsp ground coriander

½ tsp turmeric, 1 tsp garam masala

½ tsp chilli powder, 1 bay leaf

500 g / 1 lb / 2 cups potatoes, diced and cooked

a few curry leaves

For the lentils:

1 tbsp vegetable oil

1 onion, finely chopped

1 clove garlic, minced

200 g / 6 ½ oz / ¾ cup red-split lentils, soaked in water overnight

½ tsp turmeric, 2 tsp ground cumin

2 tsp garam masala

400 ml / 13 fl. oz / 1 ½ cups vegetable stock

For the raita:

200 g / 6 ½ oz / ¾ cup low-fat yoghurt

½ cucumber, grated, 1 tbsp mint

SERVES 4 | PREP TIME 30 minutes | COOKING TIME 60-70 minutes

To prepare the lentil garnish, heat the vegetable oil in a saucepan over a moderate heat and sweat the onion and garlic for 4-5 minutes, stirring occasionally.

Add the drained lentils and stir well.

Thai Chicken Curry

Ingredients

For the paste:

1 tbsp coriander seeds

1 tbsp cumin seeds

½ tbsp black peppercorns

2-4 green or red chillies

8 cloves of garlic, peeled

2 stalks lemongrass

1 bunch coriander roots only, leaves reserved

2 tbsp fresh galangal or ginger

3 kaffir lime leaves

6 shallots, peeled

1 tbsp dried shrimp paste

For the curry:

550 ml / 1 pint / 2 cups coconut milk

1 chicken, jointed and skinned

2 aubergines, chopped

1-2 tbsp palm sugar

1-2 tbsp fish sauce

juice of 2 limes

coriander leaves

SERVES 6 | PREP TIME 15 minutes | COOKING TIME 45 minutes

Pound the seeds in a pestle and mortar or in a freezer bag with a rolling pin until finely ground.

Tip into a food processor and whiz with the rest of the paste ingredients until smooth. You will only need 4-5 tbsp for this recipe, so keep the rest in a sealed jar in the fridge.

Heat a wok and add 4-5 tbsp curry paste and 2 tbsp of the cream off the top of the coconut milk and stir until sizzling.

Add the chicken and coat thoroughly in the paste. Next pour in the coconut milk and stir well.

Add the aubergines, sugar, fish sauce and juice of 1 lime and simmer gently for 40 minutes until the chicken is cooked.

Adjust the flavours with more sugar, fish sauce and some more lime juice, then serve with Thai jasmine rice, sprinkled with coriander leaves.

Shrimp Curry

Ingredients

2 tomatoes

2 tbsp butter

300 g / 10 oz / 1 ¼ cups raw prawns, peeled

2 onions, peeled and chopped

2 garlic cloves, peeled and chopped

olive oil

1 tbsp curry powder

pinch of saffron

250 ml / 9 fl. oz / 1 cup white wine

250 ml / 9 fl. oz / 1 cup fish stock

400 ml / 13 ½ fl. oz / 1 ½ cup coconut milk

1 tbsp grated coconut

salt and pepper

SERVES 6 | PREP TIME 25 minutes | COOKING TIME 45 minutes

Plunge the tomatoes into boiling water for about 20 seconds.

Peel, deseed and cut the flesh into dice.

Heat 1 tbsp butter in a pan, add the prawns and cook for two minutes.

Add the onions and the garlic and a little oil. Cook until golden.

Add the tomatoes and cook for a further 10 minutes.

Lamb and Tomato Curry

Ingredients

200 ml / 6 ½ fl. oz / ¾ cup basmati rice, rinse in cold water and drain

400 ml / 13 ½ fl. oz / 1 ½ cups boiling water

50 ml / 1 ½ fl. oz sunflower oil

400 g / 13 ½ oz/ 1 ½ cups lamb, diced evenly

1 large onion, sliced

1 large potato, peeled and finely diced

200 g / 6 ½ oz / ¾ cup chopped tomatoes

2 cloves garlic, minced

1 tbsp fresh ginger, minced

2 tsp ground coriander

2 tsp ground cumin

1 tsp garam masala

1 tsp chilli powder

juice of ½ lemon, to taste

salt and pepper

1 tbsp coriander, finely chopped

SERVES 4 | PREP TIME 25 minutes | COOKING TIME 50-60 minutes

Add the rice and a little salt to boiling water in a saucepan. Bring back to the boil, cover and simmer for 10-12 minutes. Remove from the heat, keeping the lid on and set to one side.

Heat the sunflower oil in a large casserole dish and sear the lamb in batches over a high heat.

Remove the lamb, reduce the heat and add the onion, stirring occasionally, for 4-5 minutes until softened. Add the garlic, ginger and potato and stir.

Add the spices and mix well, cooking for a further 2 minutes.

Add the chopped tomatoes and 200 ml of water, bringing the mixture to a simmer. Add the lamb into the mixture and cook gently for 30-40 minutes until the lamb is tender.

Once ready, adjust the seasoning to taste and stir in the chopped coriander. Heat the rice and spoon into serving bowls. Top with the lamb curry and serve immediately.

Leek and Curry Gratin

Ingredients

12 leeks
70 g / 2 ½ oz / ⅓ cup butter
40 g / 1 ¼ oz plain (all-purpose) flour
300 ml / 10 fl. oz / 1 ¼ cup milk
200 ml / 6 ½ fl. oz / ¾ cup crème fraîche
1 tbsp curry powder
125 g / 4 oz / ½ cup Gruyère cheese, grated
oil

SERVES 6 | PREP TIME 30 minutes | COOKING TIME 45 minutes

Preheat the oven to 210°C (190° fan) / 400F / gas 6. Rinse the leeks well, keeping one leek whole and cut the rest into rounds. Heat half of the butter in a pan and cook the leeks very gently for 15 minutes.

Heat the rest of the butter until foaming in a saucepan. Add the flour and mix well to form a paste.

Whisk in the milk a little at a time, ensuring the mixture remains smooth. Then stir in the crème fraîche. Leave to cook very gently for about 10 minutes, stirring regularly.

Season and add the curry powder.

Stir the leeks into the white sauce. Spoon the leeks into ramekins and sprinkle over the cheese. Cook in the oven for 20 minutes until golden and bubbling.

Meanwhile, cut the reserved leek into fine strips. Fry quickly in a little oil until crisp then drain on kitchen paper. Serve the gratins decorated with the crisp leek.

Curried Seafood Fricassée

Ingredients

1 packet filo pastry

2 tbsp butter, melted

100 ml / 3 fl. oz/ ½ cup dry white wine

500 g / 18 oz / 2 cups mussels

30 g / 1 oz butter

2 shallots, peeled and finely chopped

200 g / 7 oz / ¾ cup raw scallops, cleaned and trimmed

200 g / 7 oz / ¾ cup raw king prawns, peeled

100 ml / 3 fl. oz / ½ cup double (heavy) cream

juice of ½ lemon

1 tsp curry powder

salt and pepper

SERVES 4 | PREP TIME 20 minutes | COOKING TIME 45 minutes

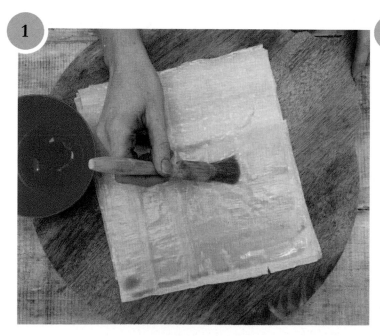

1

Preheat the oven to 200°C (180° fan) / 400F / gas 7. Lay the filo sheets out and brush with the melted butter. Turn an ovenproof bowl upside-down and grease it, then layer the filo over the bowl, shaping it round so the shell is bowl-shaped.

2

Place on a baking sheet and bake until the pastry is golden and crisp. Remove from the oven, allow to cool, then remove the bowl very carefully to leave a pastry shell.

3

For the fricassee, heat the wine in a pot and then add the mussels, discarding any that remain open when tapped. Cook for about 5 minutes, or until all the mussels are open. Drain carefully, reserving the cooking liquor and discarding any mussels that remain closed.

4

Remove the mussel meat from most of the shells, reserving a few for decoration and set aside. In a large pan, heat the butter and add the shallots. Fry until soft and translucent.

5

Add the reserved mussel liquor and reduce by half.

6

Add the prawns and scallops and poach until just cooked in the sauce – about 4-5 minutes.

7

Add the cream, lemon juice and curry powder and stir until hot. Adjust the seasoning and add the mussel meat.

8

Spoon the seafood and some of the sauce into the crisp shell and serve immediately with crisp salad leaves.

Dal, Raita and Chapati

Ingredients

For the raita:

½ cucumber

1 tsp cumin seeds

1 bunch mint leaves

400 ml / 13 ½ fl. oz / 1 ½ cups plain
yoghurt

salt and pepper

For the dal:

200 g / 6 ½ oz / ¾ cup yellow lentils

2 tomatoes, chopped

1-2 green chillies, chopped

2 tsp fresh ginger, grated

3 cloves of garlic, chopped

1 tsp turmeric

salt and pepper

2 tbsp butter

1 onion, peeled and finely sliced

chapati, to serve

SERVES 4 | PREP TIME 45 minutes | COOKING TIME 35 minutes

To make the raita, peel the cucumber and then grate the flesh into a bowl. Sprinkle with salt and leave in a colander for 30 minutes to drain.

Toast the cumin seed in a dry pan until the aroma fills the kitchen and thens remove from the heat.

3

Squeeze any excess moisture from the cucumber.

4

Then place in a bowl with the mint, yoghurt, cumin seeds and seasoning.

5

Mix together and chill.

6

To make the dal, wash the lentils and pick over for any small stones. Leave to soak for 15 minutes.

Boil 1 litre of water in a large pot and add the lentils, tomatoes, chillies ginger, 2 of the chopped garlic cloves and turmeric. Cook for 30 minutes or until the lentils are completely tender.

Mash the lentils to a rough purée.

Heat the butter in a pan and when foaming, add the onion and remaining garlic and fry until golden. Spoon the dal into a serving bowl and top with the buttery onion and garlic.

Wrap the chapattis in foil and warm in a low oven before serving.

Exotic Lamb Curry

Ingredients

3 tbsp oil

1 kg / 2 ¼ lbs / 4 ¼ cups lamb, diced

2 onions, peeled and chopped

2 garlic cloves, peeled and chopped

2 plantains

2 green mangos

½ pineapple

50 g /1 ½ oz / ⅓ cup butter

100 g / 3 oz / ⅓ cup plain yoghurt

3 tbsp curry powder

coriander

salt and pepper

SERVES 6 | PREP TIME 40 minutes | COOKING TIME 40 minutes

Heat the oil in a pan and add the meat. Cook briskly until golden-brown all over, and then remove to a plate with a slotted spoon.

Add the chopped garlic and onions and cook for two minutes. Return the meat to the pan. Add the curry powder, and mix.

90

Add 150 ml hot water and the yoghurt and stir well. Cover and cook gently for about 30 minutes, stirring regularly. Meanwhile, peel and chop the plantains into thick rounds.

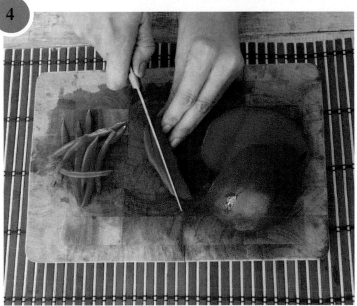

Peel and cut the mangoes into thin slices. Peel and cut the pineapple into cubes.

Heat the butter in a pan, add the plantain and pineapple. Cook over a gentle heat for a few minutes, then add the mango and season.

Stir the fruit into the curry and decorate with coriander before serving.

Lamb Red Curry

Ingredients

2 medium white potatoes

50 ml / 1 ½ fl. oz / ⅓ cup groundnut oil

500 g / 1 lb / 2 cups diced lamb

1 onion, finely sliced

1 tbsp ginger, minced

3 cloves garlic, minced

110 g / 3 ½ oz / ½ cup Thai red curry paste

750 ml / 1 ¼ pints / 3 cups lamb stock

1 tbsp brown sugar

juice of 1 lime

1 tbsp fish sauce

pepper

100 g / 3 ½ oz / ½ cup baby spinach

SERVES 4 | PREP TIME 15-20 minutes | COOKING TIME 40-45 minutes

Peel and dice the potatoes. Heat the oil in a large casserole dish over a moderate heat. Sauté the lamb until brown all over.

Add the potatoes, onion, ginger and garlic to the dish and sauté over a reduced heat for 4-5 minutes, stirring occasionally.

Add the paste and fry gently for 1-2 minutes, stirring occasionally.

Cover with stock. Bring the mixture to a simmer and cook gently for 25-30 minutes until the potato and lamb are soft.

Once the lamb and potato are soft, adjust the seasoning with the sugar, lime juice, fish sauce and pepper.

Remove from the heat and stir in the spinach until wilted. Allow to stand for a few minutes before serving.

Pork and Curry Meatballs

Ingredients

½ red cabbage, finely sliced

3 tbsp sugar

500 ml / 1 pint / 2 cups red wine

2 tbsp wine vinegar

500 ml / 1 pint / 2 cups apple juice

3 cloves

2 bay leaves

salt and pepper

2 slices stale bread, crusts removed

1 kg / 2 ¼ lbs / 4 ¼ cups minced pork

1 onion, peeled and finely chopped

1 tsp Garam Masala

10 curry leaves, finely sliced

1 tbsp dill, chopped

1 tbsp mustard

1 egg

2 l / 4 ½ pints / 8 ½ cups chicken stock

SERVES 6 | PREP TIME 35 minutes | COOKING TIME 45 minutes

Toss the red cabbage with the sugar, red wine and vinegar to marinate the day before you want to eat.

The next day, add the red cabbage and its marinade to a pan, bring to a simmer and add the apple juice.

Add the cloves, bay leaves, salt and pepper, cover with a lid and cook gently for about 45 minutes. If the sauce does not resemble a sweet and sour taste, correct with more sugar or vinegar as necessary.

Meanwhile, soak the bread in warm water and squeeze it out.

Mix thoroughly with the meat, onions, garam masala, herbs and mustard and season well. Mix in the egg and combine. Form into small balls around 6 cm in diameter.

Heat a little oil in a frying pan and gently brown the meatballs. Add the chicken stock to a pan, then reduce the heat and poach the meatballs for 20 minutes. Serve alongside the red cabbage.

Vegetable Biryani

Ingredients

2 tbsp vegetable oil

1 tsp mustard seeds

1 tsp cumin seeds

1 tsp coriander seeds

¼ tsp asafoetida

1 red chilli, deseeded and finely chopped

1 large sweet potato, peeled and diced

2 carrots, peeled and diced

75 g / 2 ¾ oz / ⅓ cup peas

1 onion, peeled and finely sliced

400 g / 13 ½ oz / 1 ½ cups basmati rice

pinch of saffron

800 ml / 1 ¾ pints / 3 ⅓ cups vegetable stock

salt and pepper

juice of 1-2 lemons

1 bunch coriander, chopped

2 tbsp roasted cashews, roughly chopped

SERVES 4 | PREP TIME 15 minutes | COOKING TIME 45-50 minutes

Preheat the oven to 200°C (180° fan) / 400F / gas 7. Heat the oil in a large ovenproof pan and fry the spices for 1 minute.

Add the chilli and vegetables and allow to lightly colour and soften, for 10-15 minutes.

Stir in the rice and coat thoroughly in the spices and oil.

Stir the saffron into the vegetable stock and pour over the vegetables and rice and mix well.

Cover the pan tightly with foil and bake in the oven for about 30 minutes, or until the rice is tender and the liquid has been absorbed.

Check to see if you need to add more stock.

Season and then pour over the lemon juice.

Just before serving, scatter with coriander and cashews.

Samosas

Ingredients

24 sheets of filo pastry

6 potatoes, peeled and diced

2 bunches parsley, chopped

2 tsp curry powder (or try ground ginger,

cinnamon or cumin)

100 g / 3 ½ oz / ½ cup fresh broad beans

juice of 2 limes

salt

70 g / 2 ½ oz / ⅓ cup butter, melted

oil for deep frying

SERVES 6 | PREP TIME 25 minutes | COOKING TIME 15 minutes

Cook the potatoes in boiling, salted water for 25 minutes until tender and then drain.

Cook the beans for 1 minute in boiling, salted water, drain and refresh in iced water. Pod the beans, discarding the outer skin.

Roughly crush the potatoes with a masher.

Add the beans and parsley and mix well.

Next, add the curry powder, lime juice and salt and mix well.

Lay the filo sheets out and brush with melted butter.

7

Using two sheets at a time, lay out on the work surface, and cut into long strips about ⅓ of the height of the filo sheets.

8

Take a strip of filo and fold the end over to make a triangle pocket and then place a large tablespoon of potato mixture in the centre.

9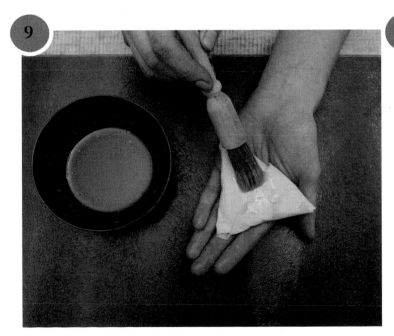

Fold the strip back on itself to form a triangle, seal and brush with butter. Repeat until all of the sheets and mixture are used up completely.

10

Heat the oil and then add the samosas carefully, two at a time. Cook until they are golden and crisp on both sides, then remove to kitchen paper. Serve with a spicy sauce or plain yoghurt on the side.

Add the prawns and stir well to coat them.

Once blended, cover and chill for 2 hours.

Heat a wok with 1 tbsp olive oil, and then add the chopped peppers. Season, then cook over a moderate heat until soft, for about 5 minutes.

Cook the noodles according to packet instructions in a large pan of boiling salted water. Once cooked, drain and toss with 1 tbsp olive oil to stop them sticking.

Add the prawns to the wok, keeping the marinade to one side, and cook over a high heat for about 2 minutes, stirring constantly.

Add the peas and cook for one minute.

Add the marinade and the rest of the olive oil.

Finally add the drained noodles and toss thoroughly before serving.

Mango Chutney

Ingredients

1 tsp cumin seeds

1 tsp fenugreek

1 tsp mustard seeds

10 black peppercorns

8 cardamom pods

8 cloves

4 slightly under-ripe mangoes

4 cloves of garlic, crushed

2 tbsp fresh ginger, grated

350 g / 12 oz / 1 ¾ cup soft light brown sugar

2 tsp salt

400 ml / 14 fl. oz / 1 ¾ cups white wine vinegar

MAKES 250 g | PREP TIME 10 minutes | COOKING TIME 2-3 hours

1

Peel and cut the mangoes into chunks.

2

Heat a heavy-based frying pan and dry-fry the whole spices and fenugreek for 2 minutes until the aroma fills the kitchen.

114

3

Add to a preserving pan along with all the other ingredients.

4

Bring gently to a simmer, and then cook for 2-3 hours until the liquid has almost evaporated and is thick and syrupy.

5

Allow the chutney to cool and then ladle into sterilized jars and seal.

6

Label when the jars are completely cold. Leave for 8 weeks to mature, before serving.

Okra Curry

Ingredients

2 tsp coriander seeds

2 tsp cumin seeds

2 tbsp vegetable oil

6 curry leaves

1 tbsp fresh ginger, grated

½ tsp turmeric

1 onion, peeled and sliced

3 cloves of garlic, chopped

450 g / 1 lb / 2 cups okra, tops removed

2 cm / ¾ " pieces

2 red peppers, seeded and chopped

250 ml / 9 fl. oz / 1 cup vegetable stock

salt

SERVES 4 | PREP TIME 10 minutes | COOKING TIME 30 minutes

Crush the whole spices in a pestle and mortar. Heat the oil in a wok and fry off the spices for 1 minute.

Add the curry leaves, ginger and turmeric and fry gently for 1 minute.

Add the onion and garlic and sweat until golden, stirring to coat all over.

Add the okra and peppers and cook briskly for a few minutes.

Add the stock and mix well with the spices. Reduce the heat and cook for 20 minutes until tender and the sauce is reduced.

If you would like more masala, add a little more stock or water and season. Serve with rice and sprinkled with a little turmeric.

Lentil Dal

Ingredients

400 g / 13 ½ oz / 1 ½ cups yellow and red lentils

1 l / 2 ¼ pints / 4 ½ cups vegetable stock

2 tsp turmeric

2 tbsp vegetable oil

2 onions, peeled and sliced

2 red chillies

1 large red pepper

1 generous pinch of asafoetida

2 cloves of garlic, chopped

2 tomatoes, chopped

1 tsp ground cumin

½ tsp chilli powder

250 ml / 9 fl. oz / 1 cup coconut milk

salt

SERVES 4 | PREP TIME 10 minutes | COOKING TIME 35 minutes

Chop the red pepper and chillies and then blend to a puree with a hand blender. Wash the lentils and pick over for any small stones.

Cook in the vegetable stock with half the turmeric for about 25 minutes or until tender. Add the asafoetida and mix well, cook a few more minutes. Drain the lentils, reserving the cooking liquid.

In a pan, heat the oil and cook the onions and garlic until golden.

Add the tomatoes, pureed peppers and chillies and add the remaining spices. Cook until the tomatoes are soft.

Return the lentils to the pan and stir well, then stir in the coconut milk and blend well.

If you would like the mixture to be runny, add a little of the reserved liquid. Season, garnish with coriander and serve with naan bread.

Turkey and Coconut Curry

Ingredients

1 tbsp vegetable oil

1 onion, peeled and chopped

2 cloves of garlic, chopped

1 green chilli, deseeded and finely chopped

2 cloves

4 cardamom pods

1 cinnamon stick

½ tsp turmeric

400 ml / 13 ½ fl. oz / 1 ½ cups coconut milk

500 g / 1 lb / 2 cups turkey, cubed

½ tsp sugar

2 tbsp tamarind paste

salt

juice of 1 lime

SERVES 4 | PREP TIME 15 minutes | COOKING TIME 30-35 minutes

Heat the oil in a pan and fry the onion until golden. Add the garlic and chilli and fry until soft but not coloured.

Stir in the spices and cook until their fragrance fills the kitchen.

Pour in the coconut milk and bring to a simmer.

Add the turkey and stir well.

Stir in the sugar, tamarind and a little salt and simmer gently for 15 minutes until the turkey is cooked.

Season with lime juice and more salt before serving.

Chicken with Yoghurt

Ingredients

For the marinade:

6 cloves of garlic, peeled

1 tbsp fresh ginger, peeled

400 ml / 13 ½ fl. oz / 1 ½ cups plain yoghurt

1 tsp chilli powder

1 tsp garam masala

1 tsp salt

For the curry:

4 chicken drumsticks

2 tbsp vegetable oil

1 onion, peeled and chopped

1 orange, zest grated and flesh segmented

SERVES 4 | PREP TIME 1 hour marinating | COOKING TIME 45 minutes

Whiz the marinade ingredients in a food processor until smooth.

Marinate the chicken pieces in the paste and refrigerate for at least 1 hour; overnight if possible.

3

Heat the oil in a pan and sauté the onion until deep gold.

4

Brown the chicken for a few minutes in a frying pan.

5

Add the marinade and cook over a gentle heat for about 15 minutes until the sauce thickens and becomes creamy.

6

Place a lid on the pan, reduce the heat and cook until the chicken is cooked through – about 15-20 minutes. Stir occasionally, topping up with a little water if the pan looks a little dry. Just before serving stir in the orange zest and segments.

Thai Prawn Curry

Ingredients

1 kg / 2 lbs / 4 ¼ cups raw king prawns

3 garlic cloves, finely chopped

6 cm / 2" inches ginger, peeled and grated

¼ tsp ground coriander

4 tsp curry powder

2 tsp paprika

1 tsp black peppercorns

juice of 1 lime

2 tbsp soy sauce

2 tbsp olive oil

300 ml / 10 fl. oz / 1 ¼ cups coconut milk

SERVES 4 | PREP TIME 15 minutes | COOKING TIME 5 minutes

Remove the heads, tails and shells of the prawns. In a bowl mix the garlic, ginger, coriander, curry powder, paprika, peppercorns, lime and soy sauce.

Add the prawns, and coat well.

Cover the dish with film and leave to marinate for 1 hour in the refrigerator.

Heat the oil in a wok. Add the prawns and their marinade and sauté over a high heat for 1 minute.

Add the coconut milk, bring to the boil and cook for a further 2 minutes until the sauce thickens.

Serve with a little fresh coriander.

Tuna Curry with Beans

Ingredients

1 onion, peeled and finely chopped

1 tbsp fresh ginger, peeled and chopped

2 cloves of garlic, peeled

1 tsp ground coriander

300 ml / 10 fl. oz / 1 ¼ cups coconut milk

2 tbsp vegetable oil

½ tsp mustard seeds

3 cloves

6 cardamom pods

1 cinnamon stick

2 star anise

2 green chillies, whole

200 g / 6 ½ oz / ¾ cup broad beans

500 g / 1 lb / 2 cups fresh tuna steak cut into large pieces

salt and pepper

juice of ½ lemon

SERVES 4 | PREP TIME 15 minutes | COOKING TIME 20 minutes

1

Whiz half the onion, ginger, garlic, coriander and ⅓ of the coconut milk to a paste in a food processor.

2

Heat the oil in a large pan and cook the whole spices for 30 seconds.

Add the remaining onion and cook until translucent.

Add the spice paste to the pan with the chillies and cook, covered, for about 10 minutes, stirring occasionally.

Blanch the broad beans in boiling water for 3-4 minutes until tender.

Add the remaining coconut milk and beans into the pan.

7

Add the tuna steak and cook for 4 minutes, until the tuna is warmed through but still blushing pink at its centre.

8

Adjust the seasoning and add a little lemon if desired before serving.

Courgette Curry

Ingredients

3 courgettes

1 aubergine

3 carrots, peeled

250 g / 9 oz / 1 cup green beans

3 tbsp olive oil

2 onions, peeled and finely chopped

1 tbsp curry paste

200 ml / 7 fl. oz / 1 cup vegetable stock

150 g / 5 oz / ⅔s cup canned chickpeas, drained

salt and pepper

6 sprigs coriander

SERVES 6 | PREP TIME 10 minutes | COOKING TIME 50 minutes

Slice the courgettes into rounds.

Slice the aubergines into matchsticks.

Slice the carrots into rounds.

Chop the green beans in half.

Heat the oil in a wok, then add the onion and cook until translucent.

Add the curry paste and cook for a further three minutes to cook out the paste.

7

Add the vegetable stock and mix well.

8

Add all the vegetables and chickpeas and cook gently for 30-45 minutes, stirring regularly until they are tender.

9

If you need to, add a little more vegetable stock or water to prevent the curry from being too dry. Season. Chop the coriander and sprinkle over the curry before serving.

Monkfish and Coconut Curry

Ingredients

1 kg / 2 lbs / 4 ¼ cups monkfish tail, peeled

2 tbsp oil

2 large onions, peeled and finely sliced

salt and pepper

3 tbsp curry powder

500 ml / 1 pint / 2 cups coconut milk

1 large bunch fresh coriander

SERVES 6 | PREP TIME 10 minutes | COOKING TIME 30 minutes

Remove any membrane from the monkfish and slice into chunks.

Heat the oil in a pan and add the onions and cook gently. Add a little seasoning. When the onions begin to colour add the curry powder. Mix well.

3

Cook for a couple of minutes before adding the coconut milk.

4

Add the monkfish to the sauce and cook gently for about 15 minutes or until just cooked through.

5

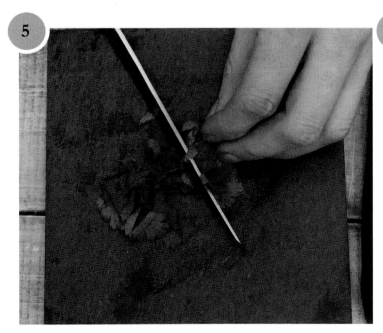

Finely chop the coriander.

6

Add the coriander at the last moment to the curry. Serve with white rice.

Veal Curry with Apple

Ingredients

1.2 kg / 2 ½ lbs / 5 cups rose veal

3 onions

3 tbsp oil

3 tbsp Madras curry powder

500 ml / 17 ½ fl. oz / 2 cups coconut milk

2 tbsp raisins

1 piece of fresh ginger

6 green apples

1 tbsp desiccated coconut

salt

SERVES 6 | PREP TIME 20 minutes | COOKING TIME 1 hour 30 minutes

Peel and finely chop the onions and ginger. Cut the veal into cubes.

Heat the oil in a pot, and then add the onions. Add the meat and cook until brown on all sides.

Sprinkle on the curry powder and ginger. Add the coconut milk and mix well.

Add the raisins. Add salt and leave to simmer gently with the lid on for 1 hour, stirring every now and then.

Meanwhile, wash and quarter the apples and remove the core and pips. Cut into thick slices.

Add the apples to the curry with the coconut, cooking for 30 minutes. Serve immediately, accompanied by Thai rice.

Curried Prawn Soup

Ingredients

400 ml / 13 ½ fl. oz / 1 ½ cups coconut milk

2 tbsp red or yellow Thai curry paste

500 ml / 1 pint / 2 cups fish stock

3 tbsp fish sauce

2 tbsp sugar

2 lemongrass stalks, finely chopped

4 Kaffir lime leaves, finely sliced

1 butternut squash, halved, peeled, deseeded and diced

500 g / 18 oz raw peeled prawns

juice of 1 lime

SERVES 4 | PREP TIME 15 minutes | COOKING TIME 35 minutes

Heat a wok and add a tbsp of the coconut milk with the curry paste and fry until sizzling.

Whisk in the remaining coconut milk and fish stock and combine well.

Add the fish sauce, sugar and mix well. Mix in the
lemongrass and lime leaves and bring to a simmer.

Add the chopped squash and cook until tender to the point
of a knife, for about 20-25 minutes.

Add the prawns and cook until pink, for 3-4 minutes.

Squeeze in the lime juice and adjust the seasoning if
necessary. Serve in deep bowls.

Mutton and Banana Curry

Ingredients

For the marinade:

150 ml / 5 fl. oz / ⅔ cup plain yoghurt

2 garlic cloves, crushed

2 tsp fresh ginger, grated

1 green chilli, finely chopped

½ tsp turmeric

For the curry:

700 g / 1 ¼ lb / 3 cups mutton, cubed

700 ml / 1 ¼ pints / 3 cups water

3 tbsp groundnut oil

2 onions, peeled and sliced

6 cardamom pods

4 cloves

10 curry leaves

2 under ripe bananas, peeled and sliced

4 red chillies, finely sliced

2 sprigs of coriander, chopped

salt and pepper

SERVES 4 | PREP TIME 15 minutes | COOKING TIME 1 hour

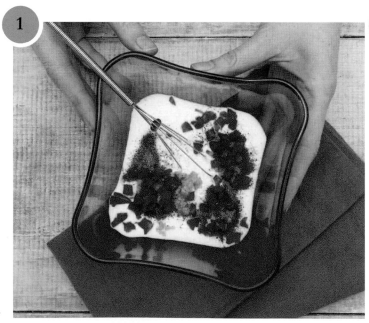

Whisk together the ingredients for the marinade.

Stir in the lamb or mutton. Marinate for at least two hours or overnight if possible.

Heat the oil in a pan and cook the onions until golden. Add the cardamom and cloves and cook for another minute.

Add the meat and its marinade, stir well, then reduce the heat to minimum. Cook for 10 minutes to allow the marinade to be absorbed.

Increase the heat and sauté the meat briskly, stirring to coat until the meat is golden. Add the curry leaves and seasoning and cook for two minutes.

6

Then add the water and cover, cook over a low heat until the meat is tender, about 35 minutes.

7

Add the bananas 2 minutes before the end of cooking to allow them to absorb the flavours.

8

Decorate with the chillies and coriander and serve.

Bombay Potatoes

Ingredients

500 g / 1 lb / 2 cups salad potatoes, halved

2 tbsp vegetable oil

1 onion, peeled and finely chopped

1 tbsp fresh ginger, finely chopped

2 cloves of garlic, crushed

1-2 green chillies, chopped

1 tsp mustard seeds

1 tsp coriander seeds

1 tsp fennel seeds

1 tsp garam masala

400 g / 14 oz / 2 cups chopped tomatoes

salt and pepper

1 bunch coriander leaves, chopped

SERVES 4 | PREP TIME 10 minutes | COOKING TIME 30-35 minutes

Cook the potatoes in boiling salted water and par-boil for 5 minutes. Drain and leave to steam dry in the colander.

Heat the oil in a large pan and cook the onion until golden. Add the ginger and garlic and cook for a further 2 minutes.

159

Crush the seeds in a pestle and mortar.

Add the chillies and spices to the pan and stir to coat, cooking for a further minute.

Add the potatoes and mix well with the spices.

Add the tomatoes and simmer for 15-20 minutes until the sauce has reduced and the potatoes are completely cooked.

Adjust the seasoning and sprinkle with coriander leaves before serving.

Aubergine Curry

Ingredients

2 aubergines, thinly sliced into rounds

pinch of turmeric

pinch of ground coriander

salt

vegetable oil

1 red onion, cut into eighths

1 tsp cumin seeds

1 red chilli, deseeded and finely chopped

250 ml / 9 fl. oz / 1 cup plain yoghurt

1 bunch coriander, chopped

SERVES 4 | PREP TIME 10 minutes | COOKING TIME 30 minutes

Sprinkle the aubergines with chopped chillies, turmeric and ground coriander.

Heat the oil in a pan and fry the aubergine rounds in batches until tender and golden. Drain on kitchen paper to de-grease.

Fry the red onion in a little oil until softened and slightly caramelized. Drain on kitchen paper.

Toast the cumin seeds in the pan until darkened and the aroma fills the kitchen. Scrape into a bowl and whisk with the yoghurt.

Warm the yoghurt very gently in the frying pan, stirring. Return the drained aubergines to the yoghurt and heat very gently.

Serve the aubergines stacked in the yoghurt sauce, decorated with the red onion and sprinkled with coriander.

Lamb Biryani

Ingredients

200 g / 6 ½ oz / ¾ cup green beans

4 tbsp groundnut oil

250 ml / 9 fl. oz / 1 cup water

1.5kg / 2 ½ lbs / 5 cups lamb, cubed

2 onions, peeled and finely chopped

4 cardamom pods

½ tsp ground ginger

½ tsp curry powder

1 pepper, finely chopped

75 g / 2 ½ oz / ⅓ cup cooked peas

500 g / 1 lb / 2 cups basmati rice

6 sprigs of fresh coriander

SERVES 6 | PREP TIME 20 minutes | COOKING TIME 1 hour

Cook the green beans in boiling, salted water for 5 minutes. Drain and refresh in iced water. Once cooled, slice the beans.

Heat the oil in a pan and add the onions, lamb and cardamom and brown the meat all over.

Add the water and spices and leave to cook gently for about 40 minutes.

Then add all of the vegetables and cook for a further 5 minutes.

Meanwhile cook the rice according to the packet instructions. Drain and add to the vegetables, stir well and leave to cook gently for another 10-15 minutes. Adjust the seasoning and serve warm, sprinkled with coriander.

Cauliflower and Pea Curry

Ingredients

2 tbsp vegetable oil

1 tsp turmeric

½ tsp mustard seeds

½ tsp cumin seeds

1 large onion, peeled and chopped

2 red chillies, deseeded and chopped

1 tbsp fresh ginger, grated

4 cloves of garlic, chopped

3 large potatoes, peeled and diced

400 g / 14 oz / 1 ½ cups cauliflower florets

75 g / 2 ½ oz peas

pinch of saffron

400 ml / 14 fl. oz / 1 ½ cups coconut milk
or vegetable stock

100 ml / 3 ½ fl. oz water

salt and pepper

SERVES 4 | PREP TIME 15 minutes | COOKING TIME 40 minutes

Heat the oil in a pan and cook the cumin and mustard seeds until they start to pop.

Add the onion and chillies and cook until golden, stirring regularly.

3

Add the turmeric, ginger and garlic and cook for a further 2 minutes.

4

Add the potatoes, cauliflower and water and stir well. Leave to cook for 5 minutes.

5

Add the saffron and coconut milk, season and leave to simmer for 15-20 minutes until the vegetables are tender.

6

Five minutes before the end of cooking, stir through the peas. Adjust the seasoning and serve.

Garam Massala Vegetables

Ingredients

3 garlic cloves, finely chopped

1 small red chilli, finely chopped

Vegetable oil

100 g / 3 ½ oz / ½ cup natural yoghurt

3 potatoes, peeled and cubed

6 small carrots, cut in half lengthways

12 cauliflower florets

2 courgettes, cut into rounds

1 aubergine, cubed

1 tbsp garam masala

1 tbsp curry powder

salt

SERVES 6 | PREP TIME 20 minutes | COOKING TIME 30 minutes

In a bowl, mix together the yoghurt, spices, garlic, chilli and 3 tbsp oil.

Cook the carrots and potatoes in boiling, salted water for 15 minutes. Drain and allow to cool. Cook the cauliflower in a separate pan of salted boiling water for 12 minutes until tender but firm.

Put all of the vegetables in a roasting tin and coat with the yoghurt mixture. Leave to marinate for one hour. Preheat the oven to 240°C (220° fan) / 460F / gas 9.

Cook the vegetables in the oven for 20 minutes, turning once or twice so they cook evenly.

Place under a hot grill for 10 minutes until browned.

Serve immediately, seasoned with salt.

Scallop and Leek Curry

Ingredients

40 g / 1 ½ oz unsalted butter

2 leeks, cleaned and finely sliced

2 tsp curry powder

100 ml / 3 ½ fl. oz / ½ cup double cream

juice of ½ lemon

salt and pepper

30 g / 1 oz unsalted butter

16 scallops, cleaned and trimmed

SERVES 4 | PREP TIME 10 minutes | COOKING TIME 20 minutes

Heat the butter in a pan and when foaming, add the leeks. Cook very gently until the leeks are soft and sweet, but not coloured.

Add the curry powder and cook for 2 minutes to release the flavour.

Stir in the cream and mix well.

Squeeze in the lemon juice a little at a time, tasting as you go and season. Set aside.

Heat the butter in a heavy-based frying pan and fry the scallops in batches over a high heat for 2 minutes on each side until golden.

Spoon the curried leeks onto individual plates and top with the scallops. Sprinkle a little salt on the scallops just before serving.

Lamb and Spinach Curry

Ingredients

3 onions, peeled and chopped

2 garlic cloves, peeled and chopped

3 tbsp olive oil

1 tsp ground coriander

1 tsp turmeric

½ tsp paprika

1 tsp ground cumin

1 cinnamon stick

800 g / 1 ¾ lbs / 3 ⅓ cups lamb, cubed

175 g / 6 oz / ¾ cup tomatoes, peeled, seeded and diced

200 ml / 6 ½ fl. oz / ¾ cup coconut milk

250 g / 9 oz / 1 cup spinach leaves

salt and pepper

SERVES 4 | PREP TIME 20 minutes | COOKING TIME 40 minutes

Peel and chop the onions and garlic. Wash the spinach leaves.

Heat the oil in a large pan and cook the onion and garlic without colouring for three minutes.

Add the spices and cook for a further two minutes.

Add the meat, spinach and tomatoes and stir well.

Add the coconut milk and season. Leave to simmer for 35 minutes, until the lamb is tender.

Once the sauce has reduced, season and stir well. Serve warm with rice.

Lamb and Bean Curry

Ingredients

4 tbsp oil

500 g / 1lb / 2 cups lamb, cubed

1 onion, peeled and finely chopped

2 cloves of garlic, chopped

1 tsp fresh ginger, chopped

1 tsp ground coriander

½ tsp ground cumin

½ tsp garam masala

2 bay leaves

500 ml / 18 fl. oz / 2 cups chicken stock

400 g canned flageolet beans, drained

salt and pepper

2 sprigs coriander leaves, chopped

SERVES 4 | PREP TIME 10 minutes | COOKING TIME 75 minutes

Heat the oil in a pan and sear the meat in batches, browning on all sides. Place in a bowl using a slotted spoon.

Sauté the onion over a medium heat until deep golden-brown, for about 20 minutes, stirring regularly.

Add the spices and cook for a further minute to release the flavours.

Add the stock and simmer gently for 10 minutes.

Return the meat to the pan, add the beans, season and cook gently for 30-45 minutes, until the lamb is tender.

Serve sprinkled with coriander leaves.

Chicken and Potato Masaman

Ingredients

3 tbsp olive oil

4 chicken breasts, cubed

1 tbsp masaman curry paste

8 potatoes, peeled and diced

500 ml / 1 pint / 2 cups coconut milk

juice of 1 lime

1 tbsp brown sugar

salt and pepper

SERVES 4 | PREP TIME 15 minutes | COOKING TIME 30 minutes

Heat the oil in a wok and when hot add the chicken. Sauté the chicken until golden on all sides for about 5 minutes.

Add the curry paste and stir to coat the chicken. Cook until the aroma starts to fill the kitchen.

Add the potatoes to the wok and stir well.

Pour in half of the coconut milk and mix over a gentle heat.

Add lime juice and stir in the remaining coconut milk until combined with the sauce.

Stir in the sugar and mix well. Cover and leave to cook gently for about 20 minutes. Serve with rice and vegetables.

Monkfish Curry with Vegetables

Ingredients

For the curry:

1 kg / 2 lbs / 4 ¼ cups monkfish tail, peeled

2 tbsp oil

500 ml / 1 pint / 2 cups fish stock

250 ml / 9 fl. oz / 1 cup coconut milk

1 tbsp red curry powder

salt

4 basil leaves, chopped

For the vegetables:

3 tbsp sunflower oil

1 tbsp sesame oil

3 carrots, peeled and diced

2 fennel bulbs, outer leaves stripped and inner leaves diced

3 stalks celery, peeled and diced

SERVES 6 | PREP TIME 30 minutes | COOKING TIME 15 minutes

Slice the monkfish into chunks. Heat the oil in a pan and add the monkfish. Cook for two minutes over a gentle heat.

Season, add the curry powder and coat the fish.

Add the fish stock and mix well.

Next, stir the coconut milk into the pan. Cook over a gentle heat, stirring occasionally for about 15 minutes.

Meanwhile, heat the sunflower and sesame oil in a wok. Add the vegetables and sauté over a gentle heat for about 10-15 minutes or until just tender.

Serve the monkfish curry and the vegetables separately, scattered with the torn basil.

Korma Chicken

Ingredients

For the marinade:

300 ml / 10 fl. oz / 1 ¼ cup plain yoghurt

3 cloves of garlic, crushed

1 tbsp fresh ginger, grated

1 ½ tsp ground coriander

¼ tsp turmeric

For the curry:

4-6 chicken thighs, skinned

2 tbsp vegetable oil

1 tsp fennel seeds

6 cardamom pods

4 cloves

1 cinnamon stick

1-2 green chillies, whole

1 onion, peeled and sliced

250 ml / 8 fl. oz / 1 ½ cup chicken stock

80 g / 3 oz / ⅓ cup warm creamed coconut

3 tbsp ground almonds

1 tsp garam masala

salt and pepper

SERVES 4 | PREP TIME 30 minutes | COOKING TIME 45 minutes

Mix together the marinade ingredients until they are blended well.

Coat the chicken thighs and leave to marinate for at least 1 hour or overnight if possible.

Heat the oil in a pan and add the whole spices and fry for 1 minute. Add the chillies, onion and a pinch of salt and cook over a moderate heat until the onions are deep gold and the chillies golden in patches.

Add the chicken and its marinade to the pan and the stock. Turn the heat down to low and simmer, covered, for about 30 minutes, or until the chicken is cooked through.

Stir in the creamed coconut and mix well.

Add the almonds and garam masala and stir until the sauce is creamy and thick. Adjust the seasoning and serve with rice.

Jalfrezi Paneer

Ingredients

250 g / 9 oz / 1 cup paneer cheese, cut into cubes

½ tsp ground cumin

½ tsp ground coriander

2 tbsp vegetable oil

1 green pepper, deseeded and chopped

1 onion, peeled and chopped

2 cloves of garlic, chopped

1-2 red chillies, deseeded and chopped

1 tsp ground cumin

1 tsp ground coriander

2 tsp garam masala

400 g / 14 oz / 2 cups chopped tomatoes

salt and pepper

SERVES 4 | PREP TIME 30 minutes | COOKING TIME 25 minutes

Toss the cheese with the cumin and coriander and rub them in with your fingers. Leave to marinate for up to 30 minutes.

Heat the oil in a pan and cook the pepper, onion and garlic until soft, stirring occasionally.

Add the remaining spices and cook for a further minute.

Add the tomatoes and leave to simmer for 15 minutes until the sauce has thickened.

If the sauce thickens too much, add water and stir well.

Add the cheese cubes, to the tomatoes and adjust the seasoning and cook for 10 minutes until heated through but still firm.

Beef Curry with Peas

Ingredients

4 onions, peeled

3 tbsp olive oil

1.2 kg / 2 lbs / 5 cups stewing beef, diced

2 tbsp curry powder

1.2 l / 40 ½ fl. oz / 5 cups beef stock

4 sprigs coriander leaves

1 kg / 2 ¼ lbs / 4 ¼ cups fresh or frozen peas

salt and pepper

SERVES 6 | PREP TIME 10 minutes | COOKING TIME 2 hours

Prepare and measure all of the ingredients. Slice the onion into thick rounds.

Heat the oil in a pan. Add the beef and onions and cook over a moderate heat until they turn brown.

Add the curry powder, beef stock and half the coriander. Season and stir well.

Cover and leave to simmer gently over a low heat for an hour and a half, stirring occasionally.

Add the peas and cook for a further 30 minutes.

Adjust the seasoning if necessary, then spoon onto a serving platter, decorate with the remaining coriander and serve hot.

Index